Dyslexia and Transition
Making the Move

Rachel Davies

Published by the National Institute of Adult Continuing Education
(England and Wales)
21 De Montfort Street
Leicester LE1 7GE

Company registration no. 2603322
Charity registration no. 1002775

The National Institute of Adult Continuing Education (NIACE) is an independent
charity which promotes adult learning across England and Wales. Through its
research, development, publications, events, outreach and advocacy activity, NIACE
works to improve the quality and breadth of opportunities available for all adults so
they can benefit from learning throughout their lives.

www.niace.org.uk

For details of all our publications, visit http://shop.niace.org.uk

Follow NIACE on Twitter: @NIACEhq
@NIACEDC (Wales)
@NIACEbooks (Publications)

Cataloguing in Publications Data
A CIP record for this title is available from the British Library

978-1-86201-712-2 (Print)
978-1-86201-713-9 (PDF)
978-1-86201-714-6 (ePub)
978-1-86201-715-3 (Online)
978-1-86201-716-0 (Kindle)

All websites referenced in this book were correct and accessible at the time of
going to press.

Printed in the UK by Charlesworth Press.
Designed and typeset by Book Production Services, London.

Dyslexia and Transition

With thanks to Mark Evans, Gilly Miller, Denise Wightman and all of the students who agreed to share their stories for this book.

Contents

Introduction

This book is for dyslexic students and people with dyslexia who are thinking about going to college or university or learning at work. It is also for the people who support them. These might be friends and family, support staff in schools and colleges or trade union reps.

The aim of this book is to provide clear information about what it's like to study at college, at work or at university in the following ways:

- It will explain how you can get support for your dyslexia.
- It will tell you how to check that you can get the support you need before you start learning.
- It will tell you about the main kinds of support that you can get.
- It will suggest some questions to think about when you are choosing where and what to study.

At the back of the book there is a list of useful terms. That is where you will also find a definition of dyslexia. Most of the information in this book could apply just as well to people with other learning differences, like dyspraxia, attention deficit hyperactivity disorder (ADHD) or dyscalculia.

There are some quotes and stories from real students in the book. These people all have dyslexia. They are all either studying now or they did so recently.

This book does not give very detailed information about how learning, courses and support are funded. The reason for this is that the details of how the government funds support for learners often change, whereas the principles on which the funding is based don't change very much. Most of the time students don't need to get involved in how their support is funded. It's only in the case of higher education (HE) that the costs of getting learning support for dyslexia should be an issue for you.

Colleges, universities and training providers have the most up-to-date and accurate information about fees, loans and other costs that relate to learning. As a student or someone thinking about doing a course you should check with these groups about money issues.

Being a 'smart shopper'

Studying can be costly. You might be paying course fees, living costs or travel costs, or taking out a student loan. In addition, studying takes up a lot of time and energy. If you are going to spend a lot of time and money on studying then it makes sense to be a 'smart shopper' to be sure that you get the best results you can.

If you think you might need dyslexia support then it's even more important to choose wisely. Getting the right support could make the difference between passing your course and failing.

As a dyslexic student you have a right to get the support you need when you are studying. There is legal protection to make sure that this happens. That's because disability equality laws apply to both education and work. You can get more information about this legal protection from the Equality and Human Rights Commission (**www.equalityhuman rights.com**). If you are a member of a trade union, they may also be able to tell you about your rights at work.

In theory, every college, university or training provider should make sure that you get all the support you need to succeed on your course. In practice, the support that you get can vary a lot. It varies for many reasons. Sometimes this is due to the size of the organisation. Sometimes it's about whether staff with the right skills are employed. Whether there is up-to-date technology can be another important factor. Sometimes it depends on when you ask for support, whether you have already got a dyslexia assessment or whether you study full time or part time.

The aim of this book is to make it clear how you can get the right support for you. It will tell you about some of the factors that might make getting that support difficult. Knowledge is power. If you know how the system works then you can find your way through it and get what you need more easily.

If you are going back to learning after a long break, or if you are thinking about your next move after school, then it's useful to know the system. The way that support works for adult learners is very different from how support works in schools. If you last studied 15 or 20 years ago then you may be very surprised by what's on offer to support you. Things may have changed a great deal since you last studied.

At the time of writing, the government is thinking about making changes to the way children and young people with support needs are dealt with in school. The British Dyslexia Association has some clear information about this on their website **www.bdadyslexia.org.uk**

Most young people with dyslexia don't need personal care or medical care at school. The amount of support they need to learn can be quite small. At present, even if you have had a statement of special needs at school, you don't need that to carry on into your time at college if you are dyslexic. More information about how the system works when you leave school can be found later in the book.

How to use this book

Don't read every page!

The book is designed so that you can dip in and out of it.
That's why there are lots of headings in each chapter. Use the
headings to find the information that is most relevant to you.

At the start of each chapter there is a box called 'Key points'.
Read that if you don't want to read the whole chapter.

Checklists

At the back of the book are some short checklists. You can
copy them or use the QR codes to access them on your phone
or tablet computer. The idea behind the checklists is that they
can help you ask the right questions about dyslexia support
when you go to an open day or for an interview. It's easy to
forget what you want or need to ask about. If you take the
checklist with you then you can make sure you get everything
you need from your visit or meeting. You don't have to ask
every question. Choose the ones that seem most relevant to
you.

Discussion points

In addition, you will find some discussion points in the book.
These are designed to help you think about key issues and

how they apply to you. Each person using this book will be in a different situation. Each person's dyslexia is unique. You need to think about what the best choices are for you personally. The information and questions in the discussion points are there to help you to do that.

You could also use the discussion points to talk about your choices with the people supporting you. You could use the spaces below some of the points to make a note of your answers.

1. Things to think about before you start

Key points

1. Get support before you have major problems with your course.
2. Think about how you like to work.
3. Think about why you are studying.
4. Think about how studying will fit in with the rest of your life.

Thinking about these things can help you choose the right kind of course for you.

Discussion point

How do you feel about having dyslexia support?

Sometimes adults have mixed feelings about asking for or using support for their dyslexia. They may feel unsure about telling people about their dyslexia. They might not want to admit that they find part of their studies hard. They may feel that they can cope alone, without any support. They might want to wait and see whether any problems crop up before they ask for support.

Often students moving straight from school into college or an apprenticeship feel that they don't want to have much support because they want to move on from how they feel they were seen at school.

It's worth saying that getting support for dyslexia as an adult in a college or university or as an apprentice is not at all the same as having learning support at school. That's because adult students are in charge of their own support; they can decide what support they are willing to accept and how much of it. They are free to turn down any support that is offered. They can also say no 'for now' but go back and use the support later on.

What's more, adults are in charge of how the support works. For example, if you have one-to-one support sessions with a dyslexia teacher at a college, you and the teacher decide together how those sessions are used. The teacher will usually make some suggestions about what you could work on or which skills you could develop further, but you can decide whether or not that's how you would like to use the time. You're the boss!

However, it's worth pointing out that it is usually a good idea to use a support service before you get into major difficulties with your studies. Preventing a problem is often easier than sorting it out once it's happened. For example, if you are having trouble managing to keep up with lots of different pieces of coursework, it's better to get help early on, so that you don't have a big pile of late assignments to deal with in one go. But, as an adult student, you're free to decide if and when you ask for support.

How do you feel about having dyslexia support?

Write your thoughts here:

General things to think about before you choose a course and place to study

The term 'dyslexia' can be used to cover a wide range of strengths and difficulties. This book talks in general terms about dyslexia and dyslexia support. When you read it, you need to think about how it applies to you personally.

If you're going to get the best out of the support that is available to you at college or university, or when you're learning at work, you need to start by understanding yourself and what works best for you.

You may have had a recent assessment of your dyslexia. It might have given you some information about areas of study that are difficult for you and some ideas about what your strengths are too. If you have had some recent learning support then you may have found some strategies that work well for you – as well as some that don't!

Discussion point

What kind of student are you?

The questions below are designed to get you thinking about your strengths and how you like to work. There are no right or wrong answers. You could use the questions to help you think about the kind of learning that would suit you best and what the best support for you would be. If you haven't been a student recently then use your experiences of work, volunteering or how you organise your home life to help you answer the questions.

Energy levels

Does your energy level stay the same right through the day and across the week?

Are there times of the day or week when you get very stressed or tired?

Do you work better by taking lots of breaks and spreading out the work, or by staying focused on one thing for a long time?

Your energy levels or patterns can make a big difference to how and when you study best. They might influence whether you study part time or full time or by distance learning. They might have an impact on how you balance studying and your working life or family life.

Exams and coursework

How do you feel about juggling several pieces of coursework at the same time?

Do you prefer to focus on one task at a time or are you happy to change from topic to topic?

How do you feel about having the pressure of an exam?

Do you have good days and bad days with your dyslexia?

The way that your learning gets assessed is very important. If you do well with the pressure of an exam but find it hard to keep up with a constant flow of coursework, it might have an impact on the course you choose.

Your life

What other responsibilities do you have in your life, apart from study?

What kinds of support can your friends and family provide while you study?

What technology do you have at home? (PC, iPad, mobile phone, etc.)

What financial factors do you need to think about?

Are you going to be living at home or moving away to study?

Will you be working while you study?

Your strengths

What would your friends or family say that you are great at doing?

Do you like to work in an unstructured, creative way?

Do you like to work in a structured, ordered way?

What kinds of study strategies have worked for you in the past?

How comfortable are you with using technology?

How confident do you feel about learning about new technology?

Think about a time in the past when you learned how to do something. What worked well for you? (This could be learning to swim, cook, change a nappy, or drive, for example.)

If you can find a way to make the most of your strengths when you study then it will help you to do well on your course.

Reasons for studying

Do you have a particular work or career goal in mind?

Do you need to get a particular qualification?

Is it more important to you to study something that you're very interested in or to gain a particular qualification?

Are you studying for fun, for work, or to help you move on to another kind of study? For example, are you doing A-levels to help you get to university?

If you have a clear goal in mind it can help you to keep going when your studies get tough.

Nathan's story

Nathan is studying Level 3 Health and Social Care at a sixth form college. In the second year of his course he decided to take an extra course, A-level Psychology. This was a subject he had enjoyed when he did his GCSEs. Nathan found that he got much better results in his main course than in his A-level. He felt that the A-level course relied too much on remembering lots of detailed information for an exam, which was not his strong point. He also found it hard to write and think his ideas through quickly enough in a timed exam, even with extra time. In contrast, his Health and Social Care course made good use of his strengths in working consistently across the year. It also meant that he could link his practical work experience to the theories he was studying.

2. Going to college

Key points

1. Colleges have lots of types of support available, including dyslexia support.

2. Support is free. You do not need to pay for it.

3. It helps the college if you tell them about the support you need as soon as possible.

4. You can tell the college about your dyslexia at any point, even before you start the course.

5. You can get support for learning, for taking exams and with using assistive technology.

How the system works

There are two main types of college:

Sixth form colleges usually focus on academic courses. For example, they often offer GCSEs and A-levels. Most of their students are 16–19 years old. You usually study full-time courses at a sixth form college.

Further education (FE) colleges usually focus on vocational courses (courses to do with a job role). For example, they may offer catering, hairdressing or motor vehicle courses. They have a mix of younger students (16–19 years old) and mature students (aged 20 or above). You can study either part-time or full-time courses at an FE college.

In addition, you may come across adult or community education courses. These are often run by local authorities or organisations like the Workers' Educational Association (WEA). Sometimes they are run at adult education colleges. They are usually short or part-time courses. Often the courses run in the evenings or weekends. Most students are adults and most study part time.

Adult education classes may have learning support services but many classes take place in small community venues. This means that it can be difficult to access learning support services if they are based at the main site. Adult education tutors are usually able – and very happy – to adjust their ways of working to suit their learners, including those with dyslexia. As your tutor is your main link with your adult education college, they are usually a good first point of contact if you need to find out about getting dyslexia support or other kinds of support.

The system for getting support in colleges is the same. Colleges usually have a department called 'Student Services' or 'Student Support'. This is where you can get many kinds of support at college, including:

- counselling
- financial support
- welfare support
- careers advice

Most colleges have a Learning Support department too ('Learning Development' or 'Additional Support' are other names for this). This is where you can find out about support for dyslexia and other learning differences.

Colleges get government funding to give support to students with disabilities, learning difficulties, learning differences like dyslexia, or those who have trouble with maths or English.

Remember:

- You don't need to pay for dyslexia support at college.
- You don't have to prove that you have dyslexia in order to get support. (This is different from university.)
- It's the college's job to find out about your support needs and then meet them, as much as they can. The college might not carry out a full dyslexia assessment to do this.

Not all colleges will offer you a full dyslexia assessment with a specialist teacher or educational psychologist when you ask them about dyslexia support. These kinds of assessment can be expensive and so colleges might offer you an 'exams assessment' or a 'needs assessment' instead. Colleges only have to assess you to make sure they meet your needs. They all interpret what that means in their own ways.

They will ask you about your strengths and weaknesses. They will assess your reading, writing and other skills. They will be trying to find out about any access arrangements that you need for exams or assessments, and what other kinds of support you will need.

You might not get 'proof' of your dyslexia in a formal report, but you should get a record of the assessment in some format. If you would like a formal dyslexia assessment and the college doesn't provide this, they should be able to tell you where you can go in the local area to get one done. Be aware that this is likely to cost you several hundred pounds. (The cost varies quite a lot depending on where you live and who is doing the assessment.) Dyslexia Action and the British Dyslexia Association are good places to start because they have groups or offices all over the country. Their details are given in Chapter 8.

How you can help before you start

Colleges are really keen to find out if students need extra support for their dyslexia. They know that if they give you the right support you are more likely to stay on your course and get your qualification. That means more funding for the college! There are usually lots of chances to tell the college about your dyslexia, for example:

- at a college open day
- on the application form
- on the enrolment form
- when you have an interview
- when you start college

The earlier you tell the college about your dyslexia, the earlier they can sort out any support you need.

It's usually much more effective to give someone support from the start of the course than to wait for them to get into difficulty before doing anything. In addition, colleges have a limit to the support they have available. The college might not be willing to say it, but students who declare their needs early often get a better choice of support. One example is timing. If you would like your support sessions to take place before or after your other classes, so that you don't need to come in on extra days of the week, it's better to ask for that when the support staff timetables aren't filled up yet! You may also find that support for full-time students takes priority over part-time students' support in some colleges.

It's really helpful for the college if you share any information that you have about your dyslexia. You might have copies of a dyslexia assessment that was done at school, at another college or for work. You can give a copy to the college. You shouldn't need to give them the original reports. If you don't have this kind of information to hand, don't worry. Colleges will assess your needs before they set up your support. They might:

- get an educational psychologist or specialist teacher to assess you;
- use a computerised screening test;
- carry out tests to see if you need special arrangements for exams; or
- assess whether technology will help you.

What types of support are available?

The types of support that you can usually get are listed below.

1. Support during classes. Someone could help with taking notes, help with understanding new words, or support you with reading and writing skills.

2. One-to-one or small group support with a dyslexia teacher. This could help you improve your reading and writing skills, develop ways to help with your memory or learn about ways to study that make the most of your strengths.

3. Access arrangements for exams. This could be extra time, using assistive technology or having a reader or a scribe. The college will usually assess your needs for these arrangements. Once an assessment has been done, the college will apply to the exam boards for approval. The college will usually have an exams office and they will make all of the arrangements each time you take an exam. You should get a chance to practise using your access arrangements before the real exam takes place.

4. Telling your lecturers about your dyslexia. Sometimes the best support you can get is for your lecturers to do something differently. That might be giving you hand outs or making presentations in a different format. It could be assessing you orally instead of asking you to write an assignment. The college learning support staff will often discuss with you what information about your dyslexia needs to be shared, and get your permission to do so.

5. Assistive technology. This could be a voice recorder, a laptop, voice recognition software, mind-mapping packages, and so on. Usually colleges will lend students equipment. You'll have to give it back at the end of your course or if you decide to leave. If you are lent some equipment, the college should show you how to use it. They should also advise you about making the most of your own technology; for example, telling you about using your phone to take notes by photographing the board in class or videoing a demonstration in a workshop. The college should give you technical support for any of the equipment that they lend you. However, the equipment you can borrow from a college may not always be the most up to date. Sometimes installing voice recognition or read aloud software can make laptops very slow. Chat to your college about the technology you have at home before you decide to borrow any equipment. Sometimes the best solution is to get software installed onto your own laptop or tablet at home, and the college may be able to help with this. Some assistive technology is also available for mobile phones; for example, spell checkers.

Sharon's story

Sharon is a full-time, mature student at an FE college. She hadn't taken part in any formal learning since school. She found out that she was dyslexic when she got to college and her lecturers noticed that she was having some difficulties. Sharon is now in her second year of study and thinking about moving on to year three.

"My first year, I didn't have a lot of support but there was a lot of support in class. This year, it's like all the doors have opened and I've realised what I'm not capable of – but I've realised that I am capable of a lot, with the help and the support of the college."

When she started college Sharon felt very nervous:

"I thought I'm just going to go to pieces as soon as I get in the classroom… If I didn't accept this help I'd have given up college in six months, trust me! … To be honest, when I first wanted to do the course I didn't know that I'd get offered any help whatsoever. I was absolutely terrified of coming to college because I had no idea if I could actually manage college."

She advises other people thinking about going back into studying to give it a try:

"I don't feel embarrassed because it's not presented that way…it's a very relaxed environment…

"The help that you're getting is so helpful, in such a big way and they understand what you're going through… the support teachers totally understand… why you can't spell that word, why it doesn't make any sense to you the way it is spelt… and that's the relief.

"[My support teacher] taught me techniques that I wouldn't even know were out there … the memory thing, the remembering my own telephone number… the way she taught me the spellings, the way we break it up. I use what I could see and broke the word down in different words."

Sharon recommends that dyslexic students make the most of the support on offer to them:

"You've got to want the help. If you refuse it and you fail or you struggle it's your own downfall, isn't it? My advice is, go for your college course, accept everything, every help, every support that you might need… Don't worry, they're never going to judge you… you'll feel comfortable and at ease doing the one-on-one or the in-class support and … you'll benefit. It'll make the journey of college a lot easier!"

3. Going to university

Key points

1. You need to apply for Disabled Students' Allowance (DSA) to get some kinds of support at university.

2. The learning support service at college or university will provide a range of support. Sometimes you can choose to get support from other organisations.

3. You need to think about support on any work placements as well as in college or university.

4. You need to think things through carefully when you are choosing to tell the college or university about your dyslexia.

How the system works

You can do a higher education (HE) course at a university and at some colleges. HE means courses like a degree, foundation degree or diploma. They can be short courses or last several years. You can study them part time or full time. Sometimes you can study from home, for example with the Open University.

The universities and colleges running these courses all provide support for dyslexic students; for example, they provide extra tutorials, help with study skills and assistive technology. In HE you need to apply for Disabled Students' Allowance (DSA) to get some kinds of support.

DSA is a grant you need to apply for to pay for your dyslexia support when you are on your HE course. You don't get cash to spend. DSA is given in equipment or in services. These are usually provided by your university or college (but not always – you can choose to spend your DSA with other organisations in some cases).

DSA is not means tested. That means it doesn't matter what you, your partner or your parents earn. DSA can cover the cost of technology and equipment, services like a note-taker, or dyslexia support sessions with a specialist teacher.

You apply for DSA through Student Finance England. If you are also applying for other student finance, they will link up the applications so you don't need to fill in the same information twice. You will need to have 'evidence' of your dyslexia. This will need to be a psychologist's report or a report from a specialist teacher who holds a practising certificate. You won't get back the cost of this assessment as part of your DSA. If you are at school or college they may pay for this assessment, but not always. It's always worth asking them though, before you pay for a private assessment.

If you need to get a psychologist or specialist teacher to make an assessment to support your DSA application, a good way to start is to contact Dyslexia Action or the British Dyslexia Association. Their contact details are in Chapter 8. They have local groups or centres where you can get an assessment done. You can find out about local psychologists or specialist teachers there too.

When your application is approved, you will get a letter telling you to go to an access centre for an assessment. This isn't a dyslexia assessment. An access centre will find out what kinds of support and equipment you will need when you are studying. They will recommend the budget and type of support you should get. If you need items like a laptop with specialist software, they will be yours to keep and you won't have to give them back at the end of your course.

It is a good idea to apply for DSA as soon as you can. It can take a while for the application to be processed and to get the access centre appointment. The sooner that you get your DSA approved, the sooner you can get the support you need. You don't have to have a place at university or college to start the process.

If you don't apply before your course starts, or you find out that you need support after the course starts, don't worry. Most universities and colleges will be willing to offer some kind of support, such as study support workshops, until your DSA comes through. They can also help you with the application process.

There are rules about who can get DSA. You can find up-to-date information here: **www.gov.uk/disabled-students-allowances-dsas/overview**

If you are planning to study a course like nursing and you are going to apply for a National Health Service (NHS) bursary then you can't get DSA. There is a similar NHS grant that you can apply for instead. You can find out about it here: **www.nhsbsa.nhs.uk/students/969.aspx**

The rules about student finance for Welsh, Northern Irish and Scottish students are different from the English system. You can find out more here:

www.studentfinancewales.co.uk
www.studentfinanceni.co.uk
www.saas.gov.uk/student_support/special_circumstances /disabled_students_allowance.htm

How you can help before you start

The following suggestions may help you before you start your course.

1. Apply for DSA. The start of your first term will be much easier if you don't have to worry about sorting your DSA out. If you apply early, your support can be in place from the start of your course.

2. Introduce yourself to the dyslexia support service. If you know what they offer and where to go for support, it will be easier to get the right support at the right time. Don't wait until you reach a crisis to find out about the support on offer. It's much harder to sort out a problem once it has happened than to prevent the problem from occurring in the first place.

3. Think about all the kinds of support you are likely to need. You may need to think about more than just studying. You may need support to deal with your money or bills or living away from home. You may need help finding your way around the campus or around a new city. You may need help with managing your time. Most colleges and

universities will have student support services that cover finance, counselling, welfare services, advice about transport, housing and so on. They are usually well advertised. If you're not sure where to go for the help you need then start with your students' union. They will tell you where to go for advice.

What types of support are available?

The kinds of support that you can usually get are listed below.

1. Special arrangements for submitting your work. This is so that your lecturer knows you are dyslexic and can take account of this when he/she marks your work.

2. Access arrangements for exams. These may include extra time, using assistive technology, a reader or a scribe.

3. Note-taking services or recording equipment. These allow you to make the most of your lectures.

4. Specialist tutorials from a dyslexia teacher. You and your tutor will be able to discuss how you want to use this time.

5. ICT equipment and software. The access centre will discuss what assistive technology will be best for you. They will take into account any special software that you need to use for your course. You should be able to get technical support for any ICT you are given.

6. Extended library loans. These will give you enough time to do the reading for your course.

7. Study skills programmes. These help to develop your skills at planning, researching and drafting writing, and to understand academic conventions.

8. Mentoring from other dyslexic students.

In addition, telling your lecturers about your dyslexia will mean that they can support you; for example, by prioritising reading lists or staggering assignment deadlines.

Discussion point

Should you tell the university or college that you are dyslexic? If so, when should you tell them?

There is no rule to say that you have to tell a university or college that you are dyslexic. You can choose to tell them (disclose) at any point when you are applying for, or studying, your course. You don't have to tell them as soon as you apply.

Remember:

- You will need to tell the college or university if you want them to give you support like access arrangements in your exams.
- The college or school will not be able to give you support through your DSA without you telling them about your dyslexia.
- Your lecturers won't be able to support you unless they know that you're dyslexic.

Some people worry that they might not get a place on a course if they say that they are dyslexic. Remember that there are laws to protect you from discrimination. Colleges and universities are also very used to dealing with dyslexic students. They make a big effort to help students who need support.

Some people applying for a very competitive course, for example medicine, tell the university about their dyslexia after they have been offered a place. Only you can make the decision about what's right for you. There is more about making a disclosure in Chapter 5.

Discussion point

Should you consider your dyslexia when you choose a course?

There are lots of different factors to think about when you choose a course. You should get as much advice as you can from school or college, or from the university you are applying to, before you decide. You may need to talk it over with family or friends. One helpful website is:
http://university.which.co.uk/advice/what-learning-support-am-i-entitled-to-if-i-have-dyslexia

Dyslexia might be something to consider when you choose a course if it affects how you perform in coursework or exams or if you have a strong preference for learning practically or visually. For example, you might:

- look at how the course is assessed;
- choose a course with a work placement; or
- decide to study part time instead of full time.

Your choice needs to fit your needs and your situation. Put your ideas here:

Discussion point

Work placements

Many HE courses include a work placement. These could be a full year placement, a series of short placements, or you might be spending more of your time in the workplace than in the lecture hall.

Work placements can be great for people who prefer to learn by doing. They give you real-life experience in your chosen career. They can help you to put your theoretical learning into context.

You may need to think about your dyslexia when it comes to your work placement. If you are having support at college or university then you may need support on your placement too. Talk to the learning support service to find out what they can offer when you are in the workplace. It may be limited, especially if you are in a placement that is a long way from your campus. This can happen with teacher training courses, for example.

Another issue to think about is your assistive technology. Sometimes you can't use your own laptop at work. For example, social work students sometimes find that they have to work on a PC at their office because of the confidential nature of the documents they deal with. It can be complex to get assistive technology installed on the PCs at your workplace because of licensing and system security. Find out about these issues well before you start your placement.

Think about the different kinds of task you will have to do on your placement. The support you need may be different from when you are at college or university. There may be more time pressure than you are used to. You may be working unsociable hours; for example, if you are a nursing student. There may be limited time to check over things that you have written.

Finally, you may want to think about whether or not to disclose your dyslexia to your work placement. As this HE student explains, not everyone has a positive experience:

"She's having a lot of difficulty in her placement at the moment… She's in a placement where she's going round people's houses to see what kind of support and funding they can get from the council… She's found that the people she works with, especially her educational supervisor … have not been very sympathetic. … They've criticised her quite a lot about her handwriting … she thinks that really she's only making mistakes that anybody makes when they're writing by hand and writing in a hurry but because the university have had to pass on the information that she's dyslexic she thinks that now they are looking… spelling mistakes, getting the odd word jumbled up… and what's more, she's said that they've been talking about it in the office."

You can put your ideas about work placements here:

Alice's story

Alice works as a Learning Support Assistant. She had some learning support at school and in sixth form college but she didn't get a dyslexia assessment. She didn't have any access arrangements made for her exams. It wasn't until she was at university that she was assessed as dyslexic.

"Throughout the whole of my education people have told me that I am dyslexic but I was never formally diagnosed until I got to university. My main piece of advice really is that, if you're in an educational institute at the moment… insist that you get tested… if you're entering university, as soon as you get there, because you don't want to do it off your own back because it's so expensive.

"I got Inspiration software, computer software, and I got a tutorial with that. I got a voice recorder for recording lectures. I would have got a computer but I already had one and I also got tested for the eye thing, where you have special colours.

"It is good to know that you've got the support of the university and it is good to know… I mean I didn't know about any of the … funding before I went … Luckily I went to a university that, as far as I'm aware, are quite good, quite supportive.

"Going weekly to the dyslexic tutor was really helpful … Quite often, when you've been told throughout your whole educational experience that you're dyslexic, it's nice to know that you don't have to do things the same way that everyone else does … I drastically changed the way I took notes… I use a lot of pencil crayons… it's much more of a mind-mapping technique… I use a lot of different colours … I don't write on white paper… really simple things like I much prefer to write with pencil than I do with pen.

"I don't think I would have chosen (my course) differently because I think the reasons for choosing my course were very far removed from really thinking about my dyslexia and I think that's how I'd like it … I think if I know I can get the right kind of support I think I'd rather [the choice of course] not be affected by my dyslexia.

"In hindsight, getting that support was really helpful… I don't think I took enough advantage of my tutorials… If I did it now I think I would try and take more advantage of that, especially now that I know more about learning support.

"Take full advantage of the things that they offer and make sure that you go to their learning support and see everything, the true range of things that are possible and that you are entitled to… and I think quite often you can shy away a bit and sort of say 'Well, maybe I don't need that' or… 'I'm not sure my dyslexia's that bad'… Maybe that's the case, maybe that's not the case, but why not try it … the funding's there for a reason… the whole point is to bring everybody to the same level and to help people who have learning difficulties or disabilities to realise their full learning potential … I think unless you try to take advantage of all these things you personally can never be sure what your full learning potential is."

4. Learning at work

Key points

1. You can get support for your dyslexia when you do an apprenticeship.

2. The kinds of support on offer can vary a lot.

3. It helps if you can tell your employer, college or training provider about your dyslexia in advance.

4. You need to think through some issues about disclosing your dyslexia to your employer.

5. When you are doing other kinds of learning at work you should get 'reasonable adjustments' made by the trainers.

6. It will help if you can give the trainers some warning about the adjustments you need in advance.

Apprenticeships

How the system works

Apprenticeships are work-based qualifications. You can study them at different levels. Most government funding for apprentices is aimed at young people. Some adult apprenticeships are also available.

Apprenticeships can be done with a training provider, through an employer, or sometimes through a college. Most of your learning is done at work. That's also where you spend most of your time, though there will be some classroom learning too. You often have to take Functional Skills (English, maths and ICT) qualifications as part of your apprenticeship.

Apprenticeships can be good for people who prefer to learn 'on the job' or 'hands on'. But you need to weigh up that advantage with the fact that you still need to do a certain amount of classroom learning and written work. You also need to juggle your working life along with your studies, which can sometimes be hard to do.

As an apprentice you can get support for your learning, including support for your dyslexia. The government gives money to training providers, employers and colleges so that they can give you this support. There are rules about the 'proof' that a training provider, employer or college needs in order to give you extra support, so it is helpful if you can take copies of any dyslexia assessment that you have had done in the past with you to your employer, college or training provider.

Colleges often have an in-house learning support team that includes dyslexia specialists, but training providers and employers won't always have the same support available in-house. This is more likely to be true if they are a smaller company and there may be some limits to the support that you are offered as a result. It really depends on the organisation that you are learning with.

Another factor that affects how you are supported on an apprenticeship is time. Sometimes it can feel like you have to do lots of formal learning in a short space of time, and that doesn't suit everyone. For example, Becky is a hairdressing apprentice. She goes to a college for one or two days a week and she spends the rest of the week working in her salon. Her days in college are very full. There is little time for her to attend extra support sessions. Several students on her course have dyslexia and so a note taker makes notes for all of those students. Becky also uses a reader for her online hairdressing exams.

Don't forget that you can still get good support from someone who isn't a dyslexia specialist. It will help them to support you well if you give them as much information as you can about what works for you. For example, if you find it hard to read documents because of the way they are presented, try to explain clearly what would make it easier to read them rather than just avoid the issue.

How you can help before you start

Find any information that you have about your dyslexia and the support you might need; for example, a copy of your dyslexia assessment. This will make it easier for the employer, training provider or college to understand what support you might need and why you need it. In addition, it may help to consider the following steps.

- Think through how you might need to be supported. You need to bear in mind that learning at work is very different from a classroom-based course. You are likely to need different support when you are an apprentice to that which you may have needed at school, for example. You also need to bear in mind that you may need different support to do your job in your workplace than you need to study. Some people find that they can carry out their job role without much support, but that they need help with tasks like doing written work or organising a portfolio for their course.

- Find out from the training provider or college how you are going to learn and be assessed, and whether there are any choices. For example, in the field of health and social care it is common to record a 'professional discussion' between an assessor and an apprentice rather than ask someone to write down what they know about a subject. Most of the time there is a lot more flexibility about how you can be assessed than you realise. Training providers, colleges and assessors often have a 'usual' way of working. That might involve a lot of reading and writing for you. However, the organisations that award qualifications will often accept a fairly wide range of proof of someone's learning. This is where having evidence of the access arrangements you can have is really helpful!

- Think through whether you want to disclose your dyslexia. This can be harder when you are learning at work. You may feel better about your training provider or college knowing about your dyslexia than you do about your employer knowing. In reality, if your training provider or college knows about your dyslexia then it is difficult for them to support you without your employer finding out too.

- Think about the time you will need for studying at the same time as you are at work. There is often some pressure to complete a course by a particular point in time. This is linked to how training providers and colleges get funded. It may have a bigger impact on you if you find it hard to juggle your studies with your job. It may also be harder if you find that you tend to have to work for longer and work harder to complete study tasks; for example, writing up a report.

- Work out what support you already have in place. For example, is there a friend or family member who can help you with sorting out your paperwork at home? Can you use your workplace systems to manage your workload when you study; for example, an Outlook calendar? Can you use your phone to take notes or collect evidence of what you can do; for example, making a recording or video, or taking a photo?

What types of support are available?

The kinds of support that you can usually get are listed below.

Support for apprentices varies a lot. It depends on the kind of job role you are in and the type and size of company that is training you, as follows:

1. Access arrangements for exams and assessments. You may have to take Functional Skills exams even if your main course is assessed through a portfolio or coursework. The kinds of access arrangements that you could get for exams

are the same as you would get at school or on a college course: extra time, using assistive technology, a reader or a scribe, etc. As always, what you get depends on your situation. You always need an assessment to work out what you are entitled to. You can apply to an awarding body for access arrangements when you are producing a portfolio or some coursework but you don't often need to do this. Your training provider, employer or college will apply on your behalf to the exam board or awarding body for permission to give you these access arrangements. They can then give you them for each exam you take.

2. Support with organising material for a portfolio.

3. Support with reading key information; for example, health and safety rules and regulations.

4. Support with writing down answers to questions and evidence of what you know.

5. More time to complete your apprenticeship or to complete some parts of the programme; for example, to finish a Functional Skills qualification.

6. Support with managing the appointments and workload that are part of your programme.

For example, Nick works for the NHS and is doing an apprenticeship in Business Administration. He gets support from his assessor. She uses verbal assessment where possible; for example, she records question and answer sessions. Nick has difficulty with the online exams that are part of his course. He was referred to a local college. They did an exams assessment so that he could get extra time and a reader when he took his online exams.

Other kinds of work-based learning

How the system works

There are many other kinds of training and learning that take place at work. These can range from short half- or one-day courses to longer courses of study. You may be studying via distance learning. You may be going to a course or workshop, or learning with a coach or mentor at work. The learning might be delivered by your employer, your union or a training company, a college or university.

You have a right to have 'reasonable adjustments' made when you are learning at work. You are covered by the same disability equality laws as any employee or learner. Most employers don't have in-house dyslexia support teams. Neither do most training organisations. You can still get support when you are learning, though, because the trainer, mentor or coach can adapt what they do to meet your needs. You shouldn't need to 'prove' that you need some changes made because of your dyslexia. You should never need to pay for any changes that are being made.

For example, a local council was re-training a large number of admin staff because their job role was changing. The staff went on a three-week in-house training course. They were then mentored in their new role by more experienced colleagues. A dyslexic member of staff phoned the trainers a couple of weeks before her course. She told them about her dyslexia and what her concerns were about going on the training. As a result, the trainers on the course adapted things for her. They gave her all of the course hand-outs in advance so that she could read them in her own time. They also offered to stay behind at the end of each day to clear up any points that she was unsure about. They gave extra one-to-one support in learning a new piece of technology.

Another example is a small company that asked a trainer to provide a one-day course for some of their staff. The company asked the trainer to provide their presentation and their notes well in advance. This meant that a dyslexic member of staff had the chance to read them on-screen at home. Everyone on the course got the slides and notes in advance so that the support could be given without making anyone feel like they 'stood out'.

How you can help before you start

Find out what's involved:

- Will you need to take notes or will you get hand-outs?
- Will you need to read anything during the training?
- Will you have to take a test based on what you learned?
- Are there any parts of the training that worry you or that you think you are likely to find hard?

Other points to consider are:

1. Tell the trainer how you need them to adapt things for you. You might need to have presentations or hand-outs printed in a particular way. You may want to make sure that you aren't asked to act as the scribe for your group during an activity. If you tell the trainer in advance then they will have a chance to make sure they meet your needs. If you don't tell them until you arrive at the training venue then it's harder for them to do much to adapt the session.

2. Think about whether or not you wish to disclose your dyslexia to your employer. As your contact with the trainers, mentors or coaches is likely to be through your employer, you need to be confident about disclosing your dyslexia to them.

3. Don't assume that the trainer knows about your dyslexia because you have told your employer about it in the past. Information doesn't always get passed on as it should. If you disclose your dyslexia to one trainer, it doesn't mean that it will get passed on to someone working with you in the future. Always check that they know what you need in plenty of time before the course starts.

Sharif's story

Sharif has years of experience as a gardener, even running his own business. When business was bad he went back to studying. He has done several construction courses so that what he is learning can also help him out in his business.

"Practical things have always been my thing… Visual, space, hands-on, that sort of thing.

"You find that your memory is different, I think. You train yourself to remember facts and figures in your head a lot more specifically than other people.

"I started off with the bricky-ing course knowing full well that the practical side of it wasn't going to be a problem… I was able to approach a tutor and say, 'I'm going to need some help with the paperwork' and he was able to pass me on to the people responsible … for doing help and support, learning support.

"When reading black on white I get a kind of a headache, at the front of my head, and it's not a headache – it's a stress, a strain, and the yellow (paper) does prolong the period before that starts.

"Computers have been one thing, I suppose because of the reading… You've got to spell things correctly… they only do what you ask them to do and if you get it wrong they'll go, I haven't got a clue what you're talking about, so I've not bothered with computers.

"It's understanding what you've been asked… I've found whilst I've been here, some of the information I've been given for taking the tests here has helped … don't spend too long trying to work out a question on a sheet. If you don't see it and recognise it almost straight away, move on to the next one.

"You need to accept the dyslexia and embrace it and then use it to further you forward… If you don't go out there and try these things and find out where your boundaries are… you're never going to be able to progress within yourself… Don't be ashamed of it… It doesn't mean you're daft, stupid or anything else, it just means that you need support, and the support is out there.

"I think nowadays the dyslexia thing shouldn't be deemed as a problem… I think you should embrace the fact the dyslexia is there as much as, not as an excuse, but it's a reason for – not an excuse for… So if you find it difficult to cope with the words or the writing or the comprehension, it's not you – it's the condition that you've got."

5. Disclosing dyslexia

Key points

1. Disclosing your dyslexia means telling people about it.
2. You don't have to disclose your dyslexia but, if you don't, it can be hard to get the support you need.
3. You can disclose your dyslexia in many ways and at any point in your learning.
4. There is legal protection from discrimination in place.

How the system works

'Disclosing dyslexia' means telling your training provider, employer, college or university that you are dyslexic. There are some good reasons for doing this:

- If you don't tell them that you are dyslexic, it is hard for them to give you dyslexia support because they won't know that you need it.

- You can only get access arrangements for exams and coursework assessments if you tell your college, university or training provider that you need them.

The choice about whether to disclose your dyslexia has to be made by you. It has to fit in with how you feel and your situation. Below are some points and information that might help you to make that choice.

You have legal protection against discrimination under disability equality laws. Dyslexia can count as a disability in legal terms. It is given as an example in the rules for education providers and employers. You can get more information about the law from the Equality and Human Rights Commission at **www.equalityhumanrights.com** or from your trade union, if you are at work.

- The law doesn't say what support a college, university or training provider has to give you.
- It does say that they have to make 'reasonable adjustments'.
- It does say that you can't be discriminated against when you apply for a course or when you are studying.

You can disclose your dyslexia in many ways. These can include:

- ticking a box on an application form or enrolment form;
- telling a member of staff at an interview or in a tutorial or meeting; or
- telling your tutor when you go to a progress meeting or parents' evening.

You can disclose your dyslexia at any point in your learning journey, starting from when you first attend an open day or apply for a course.

It is worth noting that there should be some follow-up when you make your disclosure. For example, if you tick a box on a form to say that you are dyslexic, then the college or organisation should contact you to talk about your support needs. (It's fine to say that you don't want or need any support). The follow-up doesn't always happen straight away but it should be within a reasonable time frame. For example, in colleges it's often the case that learning support staff will follow up on application form disclosures at the start of a course because not everyone who applies for a course takes up the place. But if you would like to talk about the support you need before your course starts, the college should be able to make that happen, even if it's just a phone call to begin with. It's important to be proactive. Go and ask for what you need. You are the expert on your dyslexia!

Discussion point

People are sometimes worried about disclosing their dyslexia. This can be for many reasons, including the following:

- They may just want to keep the information private.
- They may be worried about discrimination or being treated unfairly.
- They may be worried that people will judge them by a label, 'dyslexia', rather than looking at them as whole person.

Despite the legal protection that is in place, discrimination sometimes still happens in more subtle ways. One advantage of disclosing your dyslexia is that you will get an idea about how you are likely to be treated in that organisation.

One option that some people take is to disclose their dyslexia after they are offered a place on a course. Sometimes they wait until they have enrolled or the course has started. That way they can get the benefits of the support they need without the risk that they will not get a place on the course they choose.

However you decide to deal with this issue, remember that it is valid for a college, university or training provider to set entry criteria for a course. These have to be applied fairly to everyone. For example, many courses will have entry criteria that include maths or English. That's true even if the course is mainly practical, like beauty therapy or carpentry. If you want to study a course but don't quite meet all the entry criteria, it's always worth talking to the training provider, college or university to find out whether there are any ways around the problem.

These days, staff in universities, colleges and training providers are very aware of dyslexia and how it can affect someone's learning. Courses for people wanting to teach adults usually cover a range of learning differences, including dyslexia. The support services that you can access are usually well advertised. That doesn't mean that every member of staff you meet will be a dyslexia expert, but it does mean that they are likely to know where you can go for support.

Kate's story

Kate is studying plumbing at an FE college. Before she started her course she went for an interview at a different college. At the interview she got a very negative reaction when she told them about her dyslexia. They asked about whether she would be able to manage the maths and English parts of the course. She was told that she wouldn't be able to get any learning support.

Kate found their attitude very upsetting. "I've never felt so humiliated in all my life! The way they treated me… and I said to them, 'but I do have dyslexia…'. They came back and said, 'Well we can offer you the Level 2 but we think you'll struggle with the exams' … It felt like he'd already judged me, like there's no way I'm gonna pass exams.

"I just felt like, so intimidated… from that interview… It would put people off if all colleges were like that."

She chose not to take up the college's offer of a place on their course. Kate chose to study at a college where there was a positive attitude to students who needed support. Dyslexia support is built into her course. She has support in her theory and maths classes, uses a coloured overlay and has one-to-one dyslexia support sessions. She is in her second year of study and planning to move into the third year of her course soon.

6. Conclusion

Key points

1. Dyslexia shouldn't stop you from studying at college, university or learning at work.

2. You are entitled to get support for your dyslexia when you study.

3. It's a good idea to get up-to-date advice and information about the kinds of help you can get.

4. You can get advice and information from the college, university or training organisation that you are interested in.

5. You can also get information from the organisations listed in Chapter 8.

6. You should never have to pay for advice and information.

I hope that the information in this book and the stories of other students' experiences will help you to choose well and enjoy your learning, wherever you study and whatever you are learning.

7. Checklists

You can use the QR codes next to each heading to access the checklists on your phone or tablet computer when you go to an open day or an interview. This will help you make sure that you get everything you need from your visit.

College checklist

1. Can you meet someone from the learning support team to talk about what you need?

2. What kinds of support are available at the college?

3. Can you borrow assistive technology?

4. Will the college carry out a dyslexia or exams assessment for you?

5. Are there any students with dyslexia who would be willing to talk to you about their support?

6. How is the course taught? Are there lots of practical activities or is it more theory-based?

7. Do you get the chance for work experience or a placement?

8. How is the course assessed – exams, coursework, group projects, work placements, etc?

9. Do you also have to study Functional Skills? Which ones? Which levels?

10. Is there any kind of maths or English test that you have to pass before you get on the course?

HE checklist

1. Can you meet someone from the dyslexia support team to talk about your support?

2. Can you meet any dyslexic students to discuss the support they have had at the university?

3. How is the course delivered – lectures, workshops, work placements, etc?

4. How is the course assessed – exams, coursework, group projects, etc?

5. Is there a work placement?

6. Will the university still give you support when you are on your placement?

7. When you go for your interview, will there be any assessments (e.g. maths or English tests)?

8. Will you be able to have your usual access arrangements at the interview?

9. Can dyslexic students have extended library or equipment borrowing times?

10. Is part of the course delivered through online learning?

11. What kind of accessibility features does the online environment have; for example, can text be read aloud or modified to suit your needs?

Apprenticeships checklist

1. What types of support can apprentices get?

2. Will the trainers or assessors be happy to adapt what they do to meet your needs?

3. Is the time for finishing the apprenticeship set or is it flexible?

4. Are there any current apprentices with dyslexia who you can talk to?

5. How is the training delivered?

6. How much time is spent in your workplace?

7. How much time is spent doing classroom learning?

8. How is the qualification assessed – exams, coursework or a portfolio?

9. Do you also have to study Functional Skills? Which ones? Which levels?

10. Is there any kind of maths or English test that you have to pass before you get onto the programme?

8. Further sources of help and information

For information on disability equality law:
www.equalityhumanrights.com

For general information about dyslexia:
www.bdadyslexia.org.uk
www.dyslexiaaction.org.uk

For information about neurodiversity:
www.brainhe.com
www.danda.org.uk

For information about Disabled Students' Allowance and university:
www.gov.uk/disabled-students-allowances-dsas/overview
www.nhsbsa.nhs.uk/students/969.aspx

For information about apprenticeships:
www.apprenticeships.org.uk/About-Us/National Apprenticeship-Service.aspx

If you live in Scotland, Wales or Northern Ireland:
www.saas.gov.uk/student_support/special_ circumstances/disabled_students_allowance.htm
www.studentfinancewales.co.uk
www.studentfinanceni.co.uk

For information about assistive technology:

http://www.dyslexic.com

This is a commercial website. It has useful information about the types of technology available. You can look at the information without buying a product.

For information from the British Dyslexia Association about a range of assistive technology:

http://bdatech.org/

For further information about NIACE's work:

www.niace.org.uk

9. Useful words

Access arrangements

These are special arrangements made when you take an exam or complete some other type of assessment. They are there to make sure that a learning difference doesn't prevent you from showing what you know or can do. In the case of dyslexia, students are often given extra time or modified exam papers. They might also be allowed to use assistive technology or have a human reader or scribe. Sometimes you can do an oral assessment instead of a written one; for example, if you are being assessed in your workplace. In order to get access arrangements, you usually need to have been assessed by a specialist teacher or an educational psychologist.

Adult education college

This is a college that offers mainly part-time courses. Most students will be adults over the age of 19. There is a wide range of courses offered. Many adult education colleges run their classes in community venues.

Apprenticeship

An apprenticeship is a programme of learning that you do mainly in a workplace. It often includes some classroom learning too. You can do an apprenticeship at different levels and in a wide range of job roles. Most government funding for apprenticeships is aimed at younger people. There are some funded apprenticeships for adult learners too.

Assistive technology

This means any kind of technology that is used to help you deal with the effect of a disability. When we are thinking about assistive technology and dyslexia we usually mean ICT, which includes specialist software or learning packages, ways of altering the appearance of text and ways to record sound or pictures. Assistive technology can also mean practical tools like pen grips, writing slopes and tinted lenses.

Disabled Students' Allowance

This is a grant awarded to disabled students at university or on HE courses. It is there to pay for the support they need relating to their disability while they are studying. It isn't means tested. That means it doesn't matter what your financial situation is, you will still be able to apply.

Disclosure

Disclosure means telling someone about your dyslexia. That could be a college, a university, your employer or a training provider. You don't have to disclose your dyslexia to anyone. There are many things to think about when you choose to make a disclosure about your dyslexia. Have a look at Chapter 5 to help with making this decision.

Distance learning

This is when you are doing a course but most of the time you study at home, independently. A famous example is Open University courses. Sometimes you go to workshops or tutorials with other students but most of the time you work alone.

Dyslexia

Dyslexia is a learning difference. It affects how information is taken in, stored and retrieved. It is linked to a particular pattern of strengths and weaknesses. There are lots of different definitions of dyslexia. It can often be a controversial subject.

One clear definition is given by the British Dyslexia Association, which states that:

"Dyslexia is a hidden disability thought to affect around 10% of the population, 4% severely… A student with dyslexia may mix up letters within words and words within sentences while reading. They may also have difficulty with spelling words correctly while writing; letter reversals are common. However, dyslexia is not only about literacy, although weaknesses in literacy are often the most visible sign. Dyslexia affects the way information is processed, stored and retrieved, with problems of memory, speed of processing, time perception, organisation and sequencing. Some may also have difficulty navigating a route, left and right and compass directions." **www.bdadyslexia.org.uk/about-dyslexia/schools-colleges-and-universities/what-are-specific-learning-difficulties.html**

Another interesting viewpoint on how dyslexia is defined can be found at **www.brainhe.com** where Dr Ross Cooper discusses a social model of dyslexia. This fits more closely with the view that dyslexia is a learning difference and is an aspect of neurodiversity.

Dyslexia affects each person differently. Each person has different strengths and weaknesses. Some situations or tasks can cause more problems than others. People often say that they have 'good days' and 'bad days' with their dyslexia. Sometimes they can find that dyslexia has a big impact on how they study. They may need a lot of support to make sure that they can achieve their potential when they are learning. Others find that their dyslexia has less of an impact and that they need little support when studying. The subject you are studying, the way that it is taught and the way that your learning is assessed can all have a big impact on how your dyslexia affects you when you learn.

Educational psychologist

An educational psychologist is a specialist in understanding how people learn and how any disabilities, learning difficulties or learning differences can affect this. They have done lots of training. Many are employed by local councils. Some also work privately or with colleges and universities.

Equality Act

The Equality Act (2010) gathered together the various laws about equality in the UK under one heading. It includes disability equality and therefore dyslexia. The Act includes the rules that relate to education and to work. It gives legal protection from discrimination against a student or prospective student who has a disability. It also covers protection for disabled people at work. This includes the provision of training.

Functional Skills

Functional Skills is the name of the qualifications in maths, English and ICT that are part of most courses in colleges. They are part of most apprenticeships too. You can do the courses at a range of levels. They are often compulsory parts of a course or apprenticeship. They are designed to make sure that you can use your maths, English or ICT skills in 'real life' situations. They are assessed by tests or exams.

Further education (FE) college

This is a college that offers both academic (GCSE, A-level) and vocational courses (courses that relate to a job). You can study here part time or full time. Students of all ages study here but most full-time students will be aged 19 or under.

Higher education

This means studying a course at Level 4 or above. It could be a degree, a foundation degree or diploma. Higher education courses are usually run by universities. You can study full time or part time. Sometimes the courses are run in a local FE college but most courses are run at a university.

Neurodiversity

The term neurodiversity is being used more and more in UK education. Neurodiversity is a view of learning differences where people with dyslexia, dyspraxia, etc. are seen as being part of the normal range of human experience and thinking. There is a focus on the common ground shared by people with a range of learning differences. There is also a focus on the strengths that their thinking styles give rise to. People who are not dyspraxic, dyslexic, etc. are labelled as 'neurotypical'.

'Neurotypical' thinking is seen as the dominant approach in education and many other institutions. The 'neurodiverse' provide a challenge to this system. Another key aspect of neurodiversity is that it recognises that many learning differences share common features; for example, poor short-term memory. It also recognises that people tend to have features of more than one type of learning difference; people don't fit into neatly labelled categories.

Practising certificate
Some specialist teachers have an 'assessment practising certificate'. This means that they can carry out dyslexia assessments that can be used when you apply for Disabled Students' Allowance.

Sixth form college
This is a college that mainly offers academic courses like GCSEs and A-levels. Most students study full time. Most students will be aged 19 and under.

Specialist teacher
In this context, a specialist teacher means a teacher who has done extra training so that they can work with dyslexic students. Specialist teachers carry out assessments for exam arrangements. They may also carry out full dyslexia assessments.

Training provider
This is a company that specialises in work-based learning. Often this means running apprenticeships.

083203